Other titles in the series:

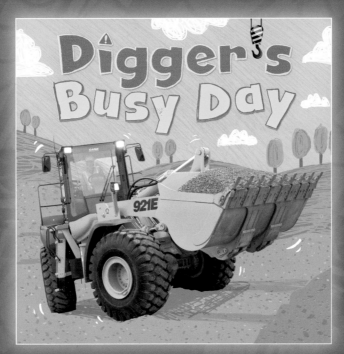

978 1 4451 4311 8

978 1 4451 4315 6

978 1 4451 4319 4

www.franklinwatts.co.uk

Franklin Watts
First published in Great Britain in 2015 by The Watts Publishing Group

Picture credits: Tony Baggett/istockphoto: 24-25; Blaze986/Shutterstock: 8-9;
Bram van Broekhoven/Shutterstock: 4bl, 12-13, 29b; Neale Cousland/Shutterstock: 20-21;
Daniel Deitschel/istockphoto: front cover; Dmitry Kalinovsky/Shutterstock: 26-27; Jason Lugo/
istockphoto: 3, 6-7; Emily Norton/istockphoto: 14-15; ownway/Shutterstock: 18-19, 28bl; Timothy
Passmore/Shutterstock: back cover, 16-17; skaljac/Shutterstock: 5, 10-11, 28c; David Touchstone/
Shutterstock: 4br, 22-23, 29c.

Editor: Melanie Palmer
Designer & Illustrator: Dan Bramall
Design Manager: Peter Scoulding
Picture researcher: Diana Morris

HB ISBN 978 1 4451 4166 4
PB ISBN 978 1 4451 4167 1
Library ebook ISBN 978 1 4451 4168 8

Printed in China

Franklin Watts
An imprint of
Hachette Children's Group
Part of The Watts Publishing Group
Carmelite House
50 Victoria Embankment
London EC4Y 0DZ

An Hachette UK Company
www.hachette.co.uk

www.franklinwatts.co.uk

MIX
Paper from
responsible sources
FSC® C104740

Big Truck's Road Adventure

Written by Amelia Marshall

Illustrated by Dan Bramall

W

FRANKLIN WATTS

LONDON·SYDNEY

All the trucks are ready
at the start of the day.
Engines are **HUMMING**,
tyres turning away.

Flicker, flicker, flash,
the headlights shine bright.
BRRM, BRRM, BRRM,
the trucks move out of sight.

VROOM

VROOM! VROOM! VROOM!
Big truck is on the move!
Its shiny steel wheels
are **fast, round** and **smooth.**

Big tanker truck is
WHIRRING and **WHINING**,
its long metal body is
SHIMMERING and **SHINING**.

BEEP BEEP

Car transporter
juggles a heavy load,
BANGING and **CLANGING**
along the busy road.

Dump truck races off
carrying all the waste.
HURRY, HURRY, HURRY,
it speeds in haste!

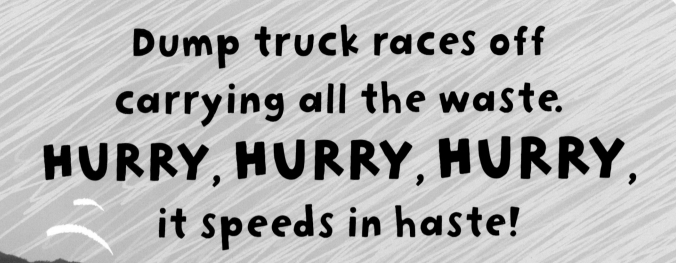

TOOT! TOOT! Log truck
trundles down the track,
heavy logs of timber
carried on its back.

Gleaming, **dazzling** rig,
shiny, red and bright,
RUMBLING down the road
all day and all night.

Long yellow crane truck
SWINGS its hook to and fro,
bumping and bouncing,
it's always on the go!

Chug! Chug!
It's road train — the
longest truck of all,
TUGGING its trailers
in a long, slow crawl.

Speedy tow truck
is **DARTING** and **DASHING**,
racing to the rescue,
orange lights flashing!

CRUNCH

Rubbish truck **CRUSHES** and **SLUSHES** the waste.
Munch! Crunch!
What a funny taste!

WHOOSH, SWOOSH, SWISH!

Delivery truck goes past,
rushing to deliver mail,
it travels really fast!

Whooosh

Clink, clunk, clunk!
It's starting to get dark.
The trucks are slowing down,
they need a place to park.

Flicker, flicker, flick,
the headlights fade away.
The trucks have all shut down
until another day.

Truck terms

Wing mirror – allows the driver to see what is behind.

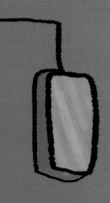

Cab – where the driver sits.

Tyres – help a truck to move fast and grip the road.

Headlights – lights at the front of the truck.

Bumper – helps protect the truck in an accident.

Exhaust – a pipe to let out gas from the engine.

Grille – vents to allow air in to keep the engine cool.

Bull bar or **Roo bar** – extra metal bar at the front of the truck.